First published in
the United States
in 1996 by
Copper Beech Books.

Printed in Thailand

Editor Jon Richards
Design David West
Children's Book Design
Designer Ed Simkins
Illustrator
Ian Thompson
Picture Research
Brooks Krikler Research
Consultant
Dr. R Levene MB.BS,
DCH, DRCOG

Library of Congress
Cataloging-in-Publication Data
Parker, Steve.
Lungs / by Steve Parker ; illustrated
by Ian Thompson.
p. cm. — (Look at your body)
Includes index.
Summary: A look at our
respiratory system.
ISBN 0-7613-0530-0
1. Respiratory organs—
Juvenile literature.
[1. Respiratory system. 2.
Lungs.] I. Thompson, Ian,
1964- ill. II Title. III. Series.
QP121.P269 1996
612.2--dc20   96-7961 CIP AC

CONTENTS

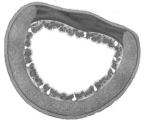

4 THE STUFF OF LIFE

6 THE RESPIRATORY SYSTEM

9 THE MOUTH, NOSE, & THROAT

10 THE LUNGS

12 BREATHING IN,...

13 BREATHING OUT

14 OXYGEN IN, CARBON DIOXIDE OUT

16 RATES OF BREATHING

19 BREATHING CONTROL

21 MAKING A NOISE

22 A BREATH OF FRESH AIR

25 CLEANING THE SYSTEM

26 SHORT OF BREATH?

28 THE LUNGS THROUGH LIFE

30 KNOW YOUR BODY

31 GLOSSARY

32 INDEX

INTRODUCTION

LOOK AT YOUR BODY! You are a complex machine, forever on the move, always going from place to place and never staying still – even if you were to sit motionless! How is your body able to keep up with all the things you want to do? Where does all the energy come from to jump about, take part in sports and do all the other things you do every single day? The answer lies inside you. Sitting within your chest are two large sponge-like organs called the lungs. Every time you take a breath, they fill with air from which your body takes an important gas known as oxygen. This gas is vital for life. It is involved in getting energy from the food you eat. This energy is what keeps you going. However your lungs are fragile objects, and from time to time need special protection to stop them coming into contact with harmful things.

EPIGLOTTIS

The epiglottis is a stiff, flaplike structure located where the throat divides into the windpipe and the foodpipe. When you are breathing, it is tilted up, allowing air to pass into the windpipe and on to the lungs. During the swallowing of food or drink, the epiglottis folds over to cover the top of the windpipe. If food were to go down the windpipe, you would choke (see page 24). Instead, it passes into the foodpipe and on to the stomach (below).

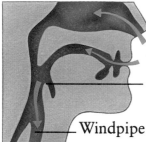

Air

Epiglottis folded up

Windpipe

Breathing

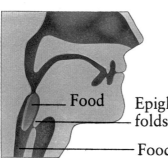

Food

Epiglottis folds down

Foodpipe

Swallowing

ADAM'S APPLE AND WINDPIPE

You can see part of your windpipe at the top of your neck, it's called the Adam's apple (main picture). This forms part of your voice box, or larynx, which contains the vocal cords that make the sounds of your voice. The larynx, in turn, leads on to your windpipe. Below this, the tube leads down your neck (right), into your chest and down into your lungs.

NASAL CAVITY

The surface of the cavity (left) is filled with blood vessels that bring warm blood to heat the breathed-in air. The surface is also covered in a layer of fine hairs (see page 25). Finally, the cavity houses the organs that help you smell.

NASAL CAVITY

Eustachian tube

Epiglottis

Adam's apple

Foodpipe

WINDPIPE

The MOUTH, NOSE, & THROAT

YOU CAN BREATHE IN AND OUT either through your nose or mouth. However, the nose is better to breathe through as the blood-rich lining inside it warms and moistens the air before it passes into the respiratory system. The inside is coated with nasal hairs and a sticky mucus lining that filters out floating dust and other particles. This warmed, moistened, and cleaned air is better suited to flow into your lungs, compared with air you may have breathed through your mouth.

Your nose also holds your smell organs which detect if there is anything nasty in the air that you may not want to breathe in.

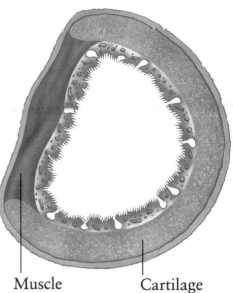

Muscle   Cartilage

KEEPING THE WINDPIPE OPEN
Your windpipe or trachea (above) is supported by C-shaped rings of cartilage. These rings ensure that the windpipe does not collapse under the pressure of the internal organs that surround it.

The lining inside the nasal cavity is soft, spongy, and delicate. It is richly supplied with blood vessels that warm and moisten incoming air. This is why a bump to the nose, or even a hard sneeze or nose-blow, can damage it, rupturing the vessels and causing a nosebleed. The usual treatment is to breathe through the mouth and pinch the fleshy part of the nose just below the bridge. Eventually, the blood should clot. But it is important not to bump or even blow the nose soon after, as this may start the bleeding again.

NOSE AND EARS
Two thin passages, called eustachian tubes, link the back of the nasal cavity with the air-filled chambers found inside each ear. These tubes let air pass through, to equalize changes in pressure. If you hold your nose, close your mouth, and blow very gently, you may feel air going along the tubes into your ears. This will make your ears go "pop" (above).

The LUNGS

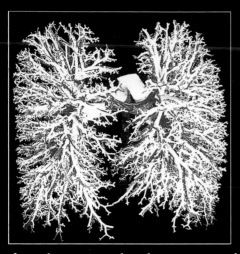

THE TWO LUNGS are like pinkish-grey, cone-shaped sponges, one on either side of the chest. Between them are the heart with its main blood vessels, the windpipe bringing air to the lungs from the nose and throat, and the foodpipe, which passes down behind the trachea to the stomach. Each lung contains intricate, interwoven networks of branching airways (above), tiny air sacs called alveoli, and blood vessels. They are all held together by a tough, elastic mixture of fibers and other substances.

BRANCHING AIRWAYS
Before it reaches the lungs, the windpipe divides into two airways, or bronchi. Once inside the lungs, these airways will divide again (right), and continue to divide into smaller tubes called bronchioles. After about 16 divisions, the airways form terminal bronchioles, which are too narrow to see with the naked eye. These airways finally end with the alveoli.

INSIDE LUNGS
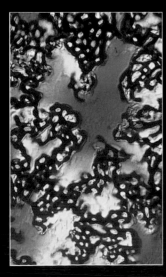

Under a microscope, the lungs appear as a collection of tiny air spaces surrounded by lung tissue (left). These air spaces are the alveoli and the surrounding tissue holds the vessels that carry blood into the lungs.

SUPERIOR LOBE

MIDDLE LOBE

INFERIOR LOBE

WINDPIPE

Lung lobes
Each of your lungs is split into lobes. Your right lung has three lobes, the superior, middle, and inferior. However, your left has only two lobes, the superior and inferior (main picture).

Alveoli
The trachea branches into two main airways called bronchi, one for each lung. These divide again, and so on (see opposite). They end in microscopic air-filled sacs, called alveoli (below). This is where oxygen passes through their thin walls into the blood (see page 14).

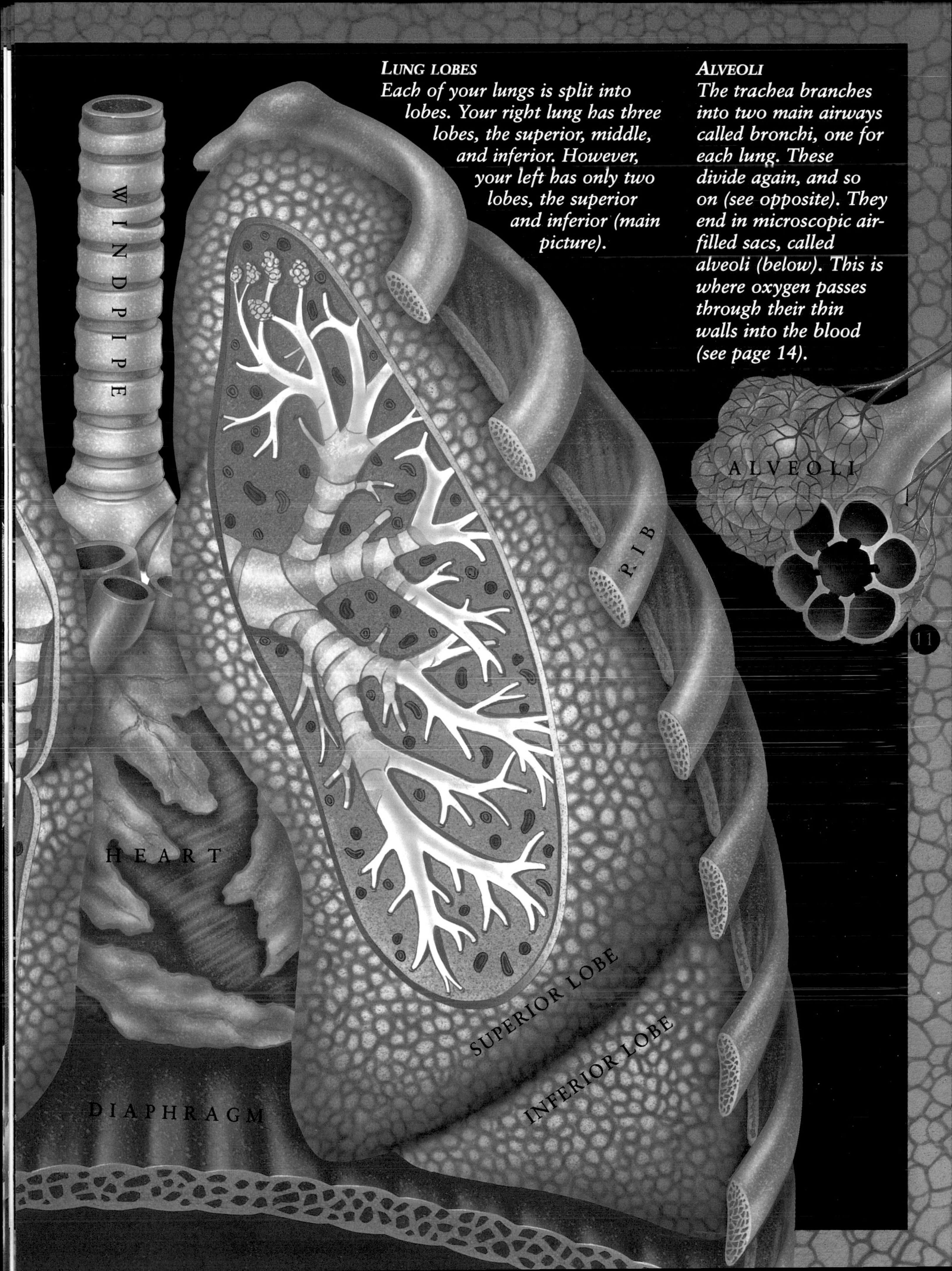

ALVEOLI

RIB

11

HEART

SUPERIOR LOBE

INFERIOR LOBE

DIAPHRAGM

The LUNGS THROUGH LIFE

THE HUMAN BODY starts its life by not needing its lungs at all. Although they are fairly well developed, the unborn baby's lungs contain no air and cannot be used to breathe. Instead, he or she has to rely on its mother for supplies of oxygen and nutrients.

Once born, dramatic changes occur, allowing the child to breathe air. These changes continue throughout the child's life, as its lungs continue to grow into maturity and then decline when he or she reaches old age.

IN THE WOMB
During the nine months of the pregnancy, the baby spends its time in the womb submerged in a watery environment, neither breathing nor eating (left). However, toward the end of this pregnancy, the baby may "practice" swallowing and breathing movements.

Mother's blood   Baby's blood

Umbilical Cord

PLACENTA

UMBILICAL CORD

PLACENTA

UMBILICAL CORD

PLACENTA AND UMBILICAL CORD
The baby's blood passes down the twisting umbilical cord and into the placenta, which connects the baby to its mother. Here the baby's blood flows past pools of the mother's blood. The two blood systems are very close, but do not mix. Instead, oxygen and nutrients pass through the narrow divide, from the mother's blood to the baby's, while carbon dioxide and wastes go the opposite way (above). The baby's blood, now rich in oxygen, flows back along the umbilical cord.

28

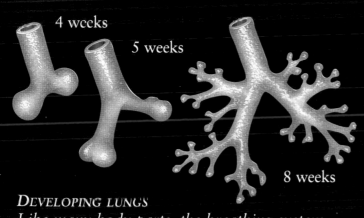

4 weeks

5 weeks

8 weeks

DEVELOPING LUNGS

Like many body parts, the breathing system develops its basic form in the unborn baby very quickly. The lungs first appear as simple branches from the windpipe about four weeks after the baby begins to grow (above). These branches become more and more numerous as the airways continue to divide. After about 24 weeks, the tiny alveoli form. By the time it is born, the baby will have only 15 percent of the alveoli that an adult has. However, these grow in size and number until the child is eight years old.

85 Years
50%

65 Years
62%

45 Years
82%

Optimum
capacity

UNBORN BLOOD SUPPLY

An unborn baby's lungs do not need a large blood supply. The vessels above the heart have a "bypass" which shunts most of the blood away from them (right). A hole between the two halves of the heart helps in diverting blood away from the lungs. Within minutes of birth, both the hole and the tube begin to close up.

Lung bypass

Hole in heart

FIRST BREATHS

As a new baby emerges into the fresh air, breathing movements will open the airways (left). A natural chemical, called surfactant, helps the alveoli to inflate. All this may be helped by pats on the back, and hearty cries from the baby.

AGING LUNGS

With increasing age, many factors reduce the ability of the lungs to absorb oxygen. This happens to the extent that by the time you reach 85 you will only be able to absorb 50 percent of the oxygen you did 60 years before (left). One reason is that the breathing muscles become weaker with age. Also, as a result of the many micro-injuries which are part of daily life, scar tissue grows in the lungs. This tissue starts to fill airways and alveoli, making the lungs fibrous in appearance (above).

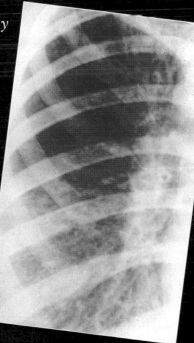

INDEX

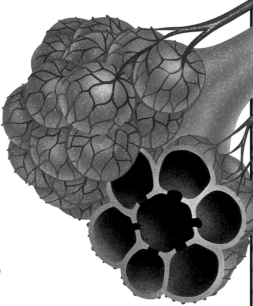

abdomen 7, 24
Adam's apple 8, 20
aerobic respiration 17, 31
alveoli 10, 11, 14, 18, 29,
   30, 31
anaerobic respiration 17, 31
blood 5, 9, 11, 14-15, 18,
   26, 28, 29
   system 4-15
   vessels 8, 9, 10, 14-15, 25
brain 7, 16, 18, 19
brain stem 18, 31
bronchi 6, 10, 11, 31
bronchioles 10, 31
capillaries 14-15
carbon monoxide 23, 26
cells 14, 15, 16, 17, 25, 31
   goblet cells 24
   macrophages 25, 31
chlorophyll 4, 31
cilia 24, 26, 31
cough 25
cystic fibrosis 26
diaphragm 6, 7, 11,
   12-13, 16, 18

energy 3, 4, 5, 14-15, 16,
   17, 22
epiglottis 6, 8, 20, 31
eustachian tube 8-9, 31
gas exchange 13, 14
gills 4, 5, 31
Heimlich maneuver 24
hiccups 13, 30
lobes 10-11
mouth 9, 20, 21, 25
mucus 7, 9, 24, 25, 26
muscles 7, 9, 13, 16-17,
   18, 19
   intercostal 12, 13, 31
nerves 7, 13, 19

pollution 22, 25
rib cage 7, 12, 18
sinuses 21, 31
skull 6, 21, 31
smoking 26

nose 6-7, 9, 10, 21, 25, 26,
   27
   pharynx 6
   photosynthesis 4, 31

sneeze 25, 30
"stitch" 16
throat 6, 10, 21, 25, 26, 27
trachea 6, 9, 10, 11, 31
tracheotomy 27
umbilical cord 28, 31
vocal cords 8, 13, 20, 21, 25
voice box 8, 20, 21, 27, 31
windpipe 6, 8, 9, 10, 11, 20,
   25, 27, 29

Photo credits: Abbreviations: t-top,
m-middle, b-bottom, r-right, l-left
3t & br, 7t, 13m, 14, 17t, 18t both
mr, 19m, 21t m, 23b, 24t, 26t,
29m, 30t both & 30b – Frank
Spooner Pictures. 3ml, 6b, 7ml,
8b, 9, 12, 13tb, 17mb, 18ml &b,
19tb, 20m, 21m, 22b, 22-23, 24b,
25bl, 26bl, 27bl & 32b – Roger
Vlitos. 4, 7mr, 8tm, 10, 15, 18,
20bl &br, 24m, 25t &br, 26m
&br, 28 & 29b – Science Photo
Library. 23t – NASA. 30ml –
Bruce Coleman Collection. 30mr
– Robert Harding Picture Library.